GETTING SHIT DONE

PRODUCTIVITY FOR THE UN-PROFESSIONAL

BY

ALICIA DATTNER

WWW.ALICIADATTNER.COM

Getting Shit Done--Productivity for the Un-professional. Copyright © 2012 by Alicia Dattner. All rights reserved. Without prior permission from the publisher, no part of this work may be copied, sold, reproduced, or transmitted in any form or format.

ISBN 978-0-9842988-0-8

Published by Unlimited, Ltd.
San Francisco

For information about permissions, updates, sales, or other questions, please contact aliciadattner.com by email at:

alicia@aliciadattner.com

Or, visit her on the web:
www.aliciadattner.com

The book's companion blog contains links to more work by the author.
www.monkpunk.org

You are not the Shah of time.

- Arnold Bennett

Dedicated to R. M.

Preface

Today a shelf, tomorrow the world.

Days seem to pass by, and we don't get done what we meant to. Boy, do we have to remember to enjoy the moment. Sometimes it can take a whole day to put up a fucking shelf. With this shelf, you can move all the crap off your desk so you can finally write that script [novel/joke/song/haiku/or long overdue moral inventory]. But you don't have the right screws. You can't find the drill. Someone borrowed the drill. You meet them for coffee. You eat a brownie and need a nap. The drill battery needs charging, so you check your email. Deleting spam. Signing another NPR petition. Facebook birthday emails. Celebrity Tweets. Ex's Tweets. Miscellaneous emails from crushes and exes about new bands and old albums (respectively). The accountant emailed you about the tax extension and

GET SHIT DONE

you have to find a receipt from 1990. You realize you've met people born in 1990 who already play guitar better than you. Get to the gym, pick up the veggie box, squeeze in a set at the comedy club. The sun has set behind Clayton Street and the shelf is sitting, waiting for your precious time. But, shit, it's too late. Sleeping roommates don't like the loud purr of an electric drill. Tomorrow a shelf, the day after, the world.

Anyway, the gist is that there are things that need doing. Receipts need filing. Resumes need writing. Clothes need folding. Things need doing.

A year ago, while reading the infamous Getting Things Done, I was fucking inspired. I was at Office Max like every other day. And Office Depot on the odd days. Three by five cards. File folders. Inboxes. Outboxes. I tacked workflow diagrams to my wall. And this system, like every other system that works, takes doing. You have to write the shit down that you're thinking. You have to look at the list and check shit off. You have to write your next 'next action' every time you complete your last 'next action'. My friend Joe says that the beauty of the system is that once you get everything collected, you can choose what not to do. It's not about getting more done but choosing what's really important. But what if it's all really important shit? Or what if none of it is?

From Getting Things Done to Getting Shit Done

Several weeks or months later, Getting Things Done devolved. It went the way of piano lessons, the wheat-free diet, and salsa dancing. It mutated into something hideous yet brilliant. It became an entirely new system: Getting Shit Done.

GSD takes less office supplies. GSD doesn't involve a PDA (or the infamous hipster PDA (the paraleptical hipster rule of law requires that one must never declare oneself a hipster. So I don't have a hipster PDA; I have a bunch of 3 by 5 cards held together with a clip.)

Anyway, today I didn't get all the shit done. I did other things instead. Really good things. I went with a friend to re-pierce her ears. Turned out they just needed to be 'stretched'. We ate a really great Vietnamese fresh chicken roll on 16th street in San Francisco. Then we bought matching pairs of rainbow socks that were free because she found a credit from the store from 2003. I also sat in the sun for a while and smelled a delicious yet delicate rose growing on the sidewalk next to my house. Getting Shit Done: The art of feeling good about doing nothing, faster.

Introduction **The Myth of Productivity**

GETTING

The art of feeling good about doing nothing, faster.

Getting Things Done vs. Getting Shit Done

THE PHILOSOPHY
Effective use of the Mind	Zen-Like Paralysis

CHAPTER ONE: AMASSING
The Mindsweep	The Brainburn

CHAPTER TWO: HEAPING
Your Shit	Other People's Shit
Sorting	Heaping
GTD Processing Supplies	GSD Processing Supplies
O.H.I.O.	N.E.W. J.E.R.S.E.Y.
(Only Handle It Once)	

CHAPTER THREE: PRETENDING TO ORGANIZE
Organize	Read Books on Organization
Actual Organizing	Fake Organizing
Brainstorming	Braintrapping
PDA	Hipster PDA
Filing System	Fuckit Files (Trash-Based)
Organized Email System	Trash Can
File-Folder Setup	Where It'll Really Go
@ Lists	Dumb @ Lists

Introduction **The Myth of Productivity**

SHIT DONE

(for dropouts of the cult organizational system Getting Things Done.)

Getting Things Done vs. Getting Shit Done

CHAPTER FOUR: THE CONTINUING HEADACHE

Mindmapping	Synapping
Weekly Review	Sleepsorting
Freeing Higher Thought	Cultivate Cerebral Hypoefficiency
Daily Review	Paradoxical Efficiency of Indecision
Concrete Goals	Abstract Goals

CHAPTER FIVE: TAKING (NON)ACTION

Hyper-Productivity	Rationalization: Leatherman of Procrastination
Two-minute Action	Twenty-minute Action
Do It Now	Procrastination
Freeing Higher Thought	Shock Value
Incremental Progression	Incremental Regression
One Thing at a Time	GSD During Work
Multi-tasking	Ultra-tasking
Delegate	Relegate

THE REAL VALUE OF GSD

Greater Productivity	Posterity
Ultra-efficiency	Value of Emptiness

Getting Shit Done Tools For Unprofessionals

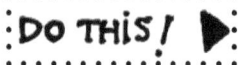 **GSD Personality Typing**

Clear your mind and without thinking, return to the last page. Look at both columns, and put a check next to the activity that feels preferable to your genuine self.

Add one point for each check in the right-hand column.

      Total in this column: _____

If you scored:

0-9: Go ahead, keep your tie on! A fun thing you could do so as not alarm your colleagues is take the cover of Getting Things Done and put it on this book, kind of like in school when putting Mad Magazine inside the Biology textbook. Drinking in this book will likely produce in the back of your throat a smug sensation of superiority over the weak-minded. Wash it down with a bit of Nietzsche. This might be you:

10-19: Loosen the tie! I sense some ambivalence. Ok, I can't actually sense what you're feeling, but I'm imagining you, dear reader, holding this book in your hands, having , wondering, "Can I really let go of Being Organized? I need to be in control. I can't just magically not have receipts or mail any more. Come on, I can't just dive into some oblivion where I stop thinking and worrying about how everything will get done. Or could I…?" Perhaps reading this book will lend you the confidence to take that leap. This might be you:

TIMELINE → DONE.
(ABOUT HALF AN HOUR.)

20-29: Do you even own a tie? (I don't. Ok, at one point in high school I was trying this Diane Keaton woman-tie-thing, but I ended up looking more like Buster Keaton.) Anyway, I think you and I are on the same page (which would make sense, because I've just written this book about the answers you chose and also because I'm writing this page right now and you're also reading it right now, which is a kind of incredible time-space conundrum!). We are going to share some more very interesting coincidences. This might be you:

Introduction The Myth of Productivity

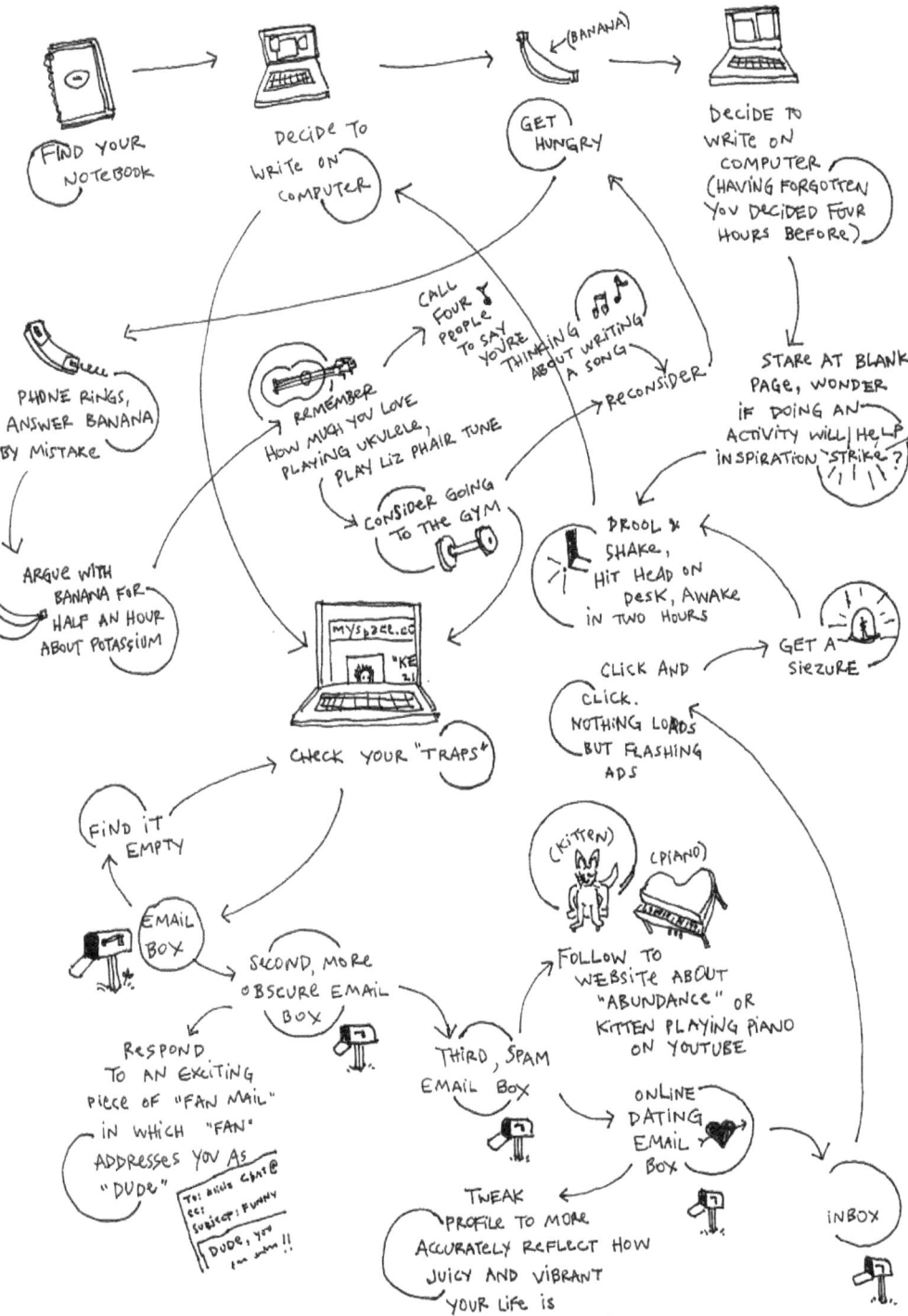

The magic of Getting Shit Done

The magic is that once you've begun to incorporate the system into your life wholesale, you can begin to zap your mind into the upper echelons of thought! This process will move your whole way of navigating the world **from future-tripping to future-flipping!** You will begin to understand empirically what it's like to enter those flashing Super-Mario states of invincibility. While it's helpful to measure time in conventional units, thinking about time in new ways can radically shift the way we relate to the clock. Here are some examples of metaphorical future time-units. Where do you see yourself in the future?

Zen-Like Paralysis

What is at the heart of Getting Shit Done? It's a whole life-strategy of collecting in front of you every task, every obligation, every to-do, to-buy, to-eat, to-fix, every phone call, email, and letter you want to write, every career possibility, every brilliant scheme or invention (you could invent the next shoehorn!), Every thought on activities you'd like to do with your children (or future children), and every wish and aspiration for each level of your life IN ORDER TO ACHIEVE a ZEN-LIKE PARALYSIS of the bodymind that, nurtured and indulged deeply

Introduction **The Myth of Productivity**

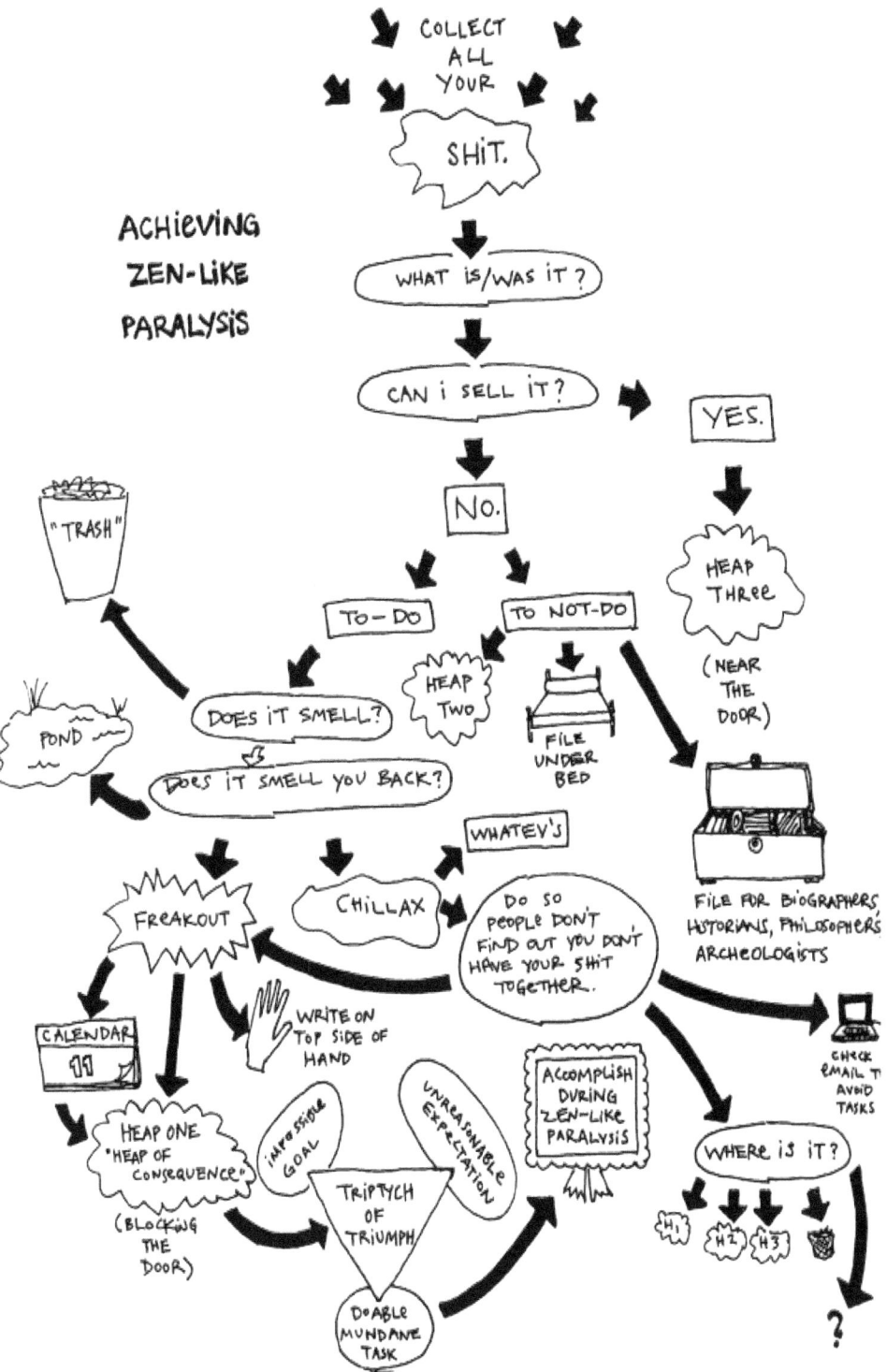

to its conclusion, leads to a profound acceptance of death and an instense natural high.

The Myth of Productivity

What is productivity? When you hear the stats on NPR, 'U.S. Productivity down .06 percent', what does that mean? How exactly does one measure productivity  *to the hundredth of a percentile? Is the boss standing behind you with a stopwatch? 'What the fuck, Fran? Can't you hit the start button sooner? You coulda had the fax number ready, you could have skipped the cover page, you coulda put the coffee down for three seconds. There's a kid in India who wants your job and is willing to work for a third of what you make. I heard about these Americans making "bank" in India as dialect coaches. Who uses a fax machine anymore, Fran? Anyway, so, you wanna get some dinner after work, Fran? I know this place downtown, makes a great curry… I thought maybe…'*

What is productivity? It's a measure of how productive we are being. What is being productive? According to the corporate definition of being productive, it's doing whatever you're being paid to do, better and faster. And the productivity rate, much like cancer or the population, is always expected to rise. But how? We're at war, so we've got to keep bringing home the Benjamins. Well, I guess we have the Benjamins already, but we have to spend them so we can earn them back, triumphantly, kind of like our own 'Private Benjamins' overseas. But so anyway, we, the united states, can no longer grow food cheaper, make cars cheaper,  *answer DSL questions cheaper. We don't have the oil, we don't have the trees (well, not anymore), and we don't have the four-year-olds who can sew. We worked our asses off for a couple centuries, and now we've reached our maximum productivity level in all these areas. What is our now the main export of the United States? It's cultural and intellectual capital. What's this mean for "America"? We're at war. IT'S NOW OUR JOB to create cultural and intellectual capital. Let me reiterate: it's now our job to write book after book reiterating the principles of Buddhism and its application in dating, Judaism, addiction, and rage, (because sitting and meditating for an hour would annoy the fuck out of us and we'd prefer to read about it). It's now OUR JOB to print postcards of Barbie dolls in compromising positions, to choreograph new dance routines for celebrities on reality shows, to grow medical marijuana so certain musicians can write and record songs about smoking the blunt and certain comedians can think of funny shit to perform on stage (which they couldn't think of without drugs because standardized tests dulled their imagination and blocked their unconscious minds). It's also our job to write blogs about what we ate after breakfast but before lunch and our job to tell the world how it made us feel. Our job to write plays about precarious priests and movies about gay cowboys. Our job to think up new ways to feel old and look young and write magazine articles about it. Our job to re-invent holidays that sell greeting cards and guilt and enough chocolate to drown the emotions triggered by people celebrating (un)said holidays. And it's our job to produce more and more technically complicated yet intellectually and textually simple porn every day. And it's also our job to criticize our job as long as we can sell a book or a movie about it.*

We must. But again, why? It is OUR SOMBER BURDEN to create the intellectual property that will drive the U.S. economy in order to pay the interest on our international loans in order to honor our monetary agreements which drive the world economy so that we all have jobs so we can earn a living so we can buy gas so we can drive so we can get to work so we can pay for the doctors who scrape out our arteries and tuck our tummies so we can eat more shit but still marry someone who will buy us iPods, lipstick, bottled water, Haagendasz, organic micro greens, hoodia, DVDs, hybrid SUVs, plasma TVs, Big Macs, iMacs, guns, winter coats, OFFICE SUPPLIES, books on Buddhist meditation, and if we're lucky we can have kids to buy stuff for, and all of these NEEDS CREATE EVENTS in our lives, which makes us feel VERY PRODUCTIVE!

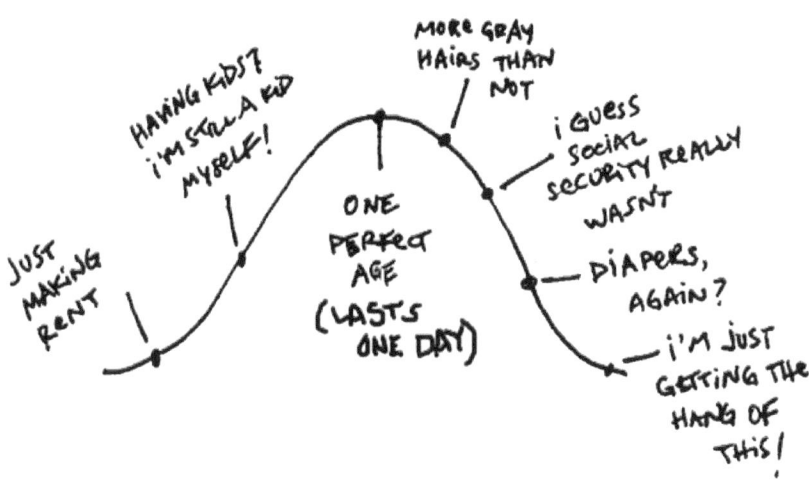

CHAPTER ONE:
AMASSING

GET
SHIT
DONE

The Brainburn

As David Allen suggests in *Getting Things Done*, the sure way to a pure mind is to empty it of open loops. Open loops are incomplete processes that tether the mind to limitations like the string of a balloon to a child on a midway pony who is doomed to tread in circles for the rest of its days, trampling and killing the grass under its hooves and wearing a groove in the dirt below.

Fake Meditation

Do you fake meditate? And by that I mean, do you tell your friends you meditate? Do you sit for half an hour each day in a lotus position, with a look of calm scrawled over your face, mind wandering on an infantile rampage through the delicate and subtle hurts of a suburban childhood, through the guest-list for your imaginary wedding, the foods you will not eat when you embark upon your cleansing diet? Good. Fake meditation is good preparation for real meditation. You've achieved the exterior discipline of this activity. You're headed in the right direction. Now add the continual letting go of thoughts and the continual return to the breath and the sensations you're feeling. Add the true equanimity that comes while feeling each sensation entirely, and letting it pass.

Fake Organization

Fake meditation is like fake organization. I'm calling your bluff. Today. Now. You put shit in files, you label shit, you never really throw shit away. Your desk may be clear, but your mind is still imprisoned.

Before you read on, I want to communicate to you the sense of urgency you must feel in order to fully commit to this process and thus succeed at getting shit done. What we're really looking at here is liberation from the bondage of self. You are reading this book (yes, YOU) because you sense there is something more to life than what you've experienced up to now. An old part of you dies now so that you may begin to truly live. Scary? The consequences of not doing so now are that you may well actually die leaving life unlived. Popsicles unsucked. Oceans unswum. Roses unsmelled. Babies unkissed. Fire unbreathed. Songs unung. Lovers unsexed. Tears uncried. {Dishes unwashed (although dishes are suddenly seeming inconsequential).} If you don't start now, who knows how much more time you'll lose? But if you do, the promise of each new moment is infinite possibility.

To Teather, or Not to Teather?

There is a chain of events that causes your splendidly planned organizational system to purr like a finely tuned Porche or sputter and clunk like a Chevy Cavalier. Can you afford to be Cavalier about the brief time you have on this earth? Never mind that. The question is: after all this work organizing everything, are you actually getting shit done now, and if not, why not? Have you streamlined the seven hours of work you used to do into one hour in order

Time is nature's way of keeping everything from happening all at once.
    -Woody Allen

to spend six hours staring at your thumbs? Or do you now know exactly what each next action is and everything is so clear it's scary? Have you gotten so clear you've thrown the action list out your window, for fear you might actually get all your shit done? What happens if you do get everything done? What will tether you to this earthly realm? If there's nothing more for you to do, will you still have a purpose? It's ok, you didn't have a purpose in the first place–at least, not one that's fulfilled by the items on your action list… but I digress.

INBOX / OUTBOX

It should be clear that it's not necessary to close all open loops, rather simply that you put a system in place which the mind absolutely trusts that will allow it to truly empty itself of concerns and allow you the freedom of original thought.

The Collection Process and the Brainburn

Your inbox is the gate through which all open loops

pass. Collect every open loop in your life into your inbox. This includes all documents, bills, business cards, sentimental items, lists, etc. And to make the sorting process a little less difficult, throw in some easy stuff for your to sort, like blank pieces of paper, rocks, leaves, etc. It's a nice break when you come to a rock and you can just say, "Well, that's easy! That goes outside on the ground." And you feel as if you've accomplished something. If you have open loops which are not represented by an object or document, write them on a piece of paper and put them in your inbox. You are now signaling to the mind that a comprehensive shift is occurring, teaching your mind the system.

 **The Brainburn**

Gather all the items you've collected in your inbox. Sort into heaps. Pile together the entire inbox you've created. Collect eight pieces of 2 x 4, a box of matches, and a can of lighter fluid. Ignite the folder system on fire, and watch the system combust. Burn completely. This will signal your mind that open loops are no longer a concern.

THE BRAINBURN

Ignoring the Important Stuff

There are lots of ways to ignore the very real need to get shit done. For example, begin to think about things that never would have bothered you in the past, and cultivate fear and worry surrounding their existence or non-existence. Did you know your keyboard can have up to 25,000 germs lurking on each square inch? It's never a better time to get out a cotton swab and some rubbing alcohol and drill at some hard-to-reach crevices. It could be almost as satisfying as squeezing your zits.

If you're more of an optimist than a pessimist, you

can ignore your need to get shit done by pondering and exploring creative ideas. Google interesting websites about interesting people. There's that cool website about going outside and setting your books free like white doves at a magic show. You put a tracking number on your book and then you put it on a park bench or a bus or in a mailbox and then see who picks it up and reads it. Then you can track your book if someone finds it and registers it on the internet. There are a million more neat websites to visit.

"Sometimes it feels good to take your bills out and sort of rearrange them so the most important ones are on top, and maybe write on the back of my hand that I should take that driver's ed test to erase the point off my license. But also, I can think about how much time I still have before I really need to get that shit done.

Isn't it time for a snack yet? All this considering cleaning, thinking about doing laundry, and planning to paying bills makes a gal hungry! How about a walk to the cafe for a pain au chocolat? Mmm! Talk about a pleasure trap!"

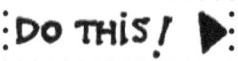 **Google Your Life Away!**

Timesuck for Beginners: 50 Great Phrases to Google while you're waiting for life to finally, magically become the way you want it! Bonus points if you can justify your search.

1. your name
2. your name + Brad Pitt/Angelina Jolie
3. your name + your partner
4. your name + your ex
5. your name + your crush
6. your name (in Google Images)
7. set books free
8. flash bake oven + pizza + cook time
9. free energy machine
10. conspiracy theories
11. conspiracy theories + your name
12. nationalized healthcare obama
13. england dental care
14. dentists mumbai
15. goa beach rave
16. san francisco rave
17. are there still raves in US
18. MDMA
19. big brother conspiracy theories
20. guiness book + smallest camera

21. guiness book + smallest human
22. guiness book + smallest baby (Google images)
23. guiness book + most sex
24. sex
25. coconut rice recipe
26. chess + steroids
27. getting things done
28. getting shit done
29. alicia dattner (what? what?)
30. 43 folders lifehack
31. what is a timesuck
32. polyphasic sleep
33. lucid dreaming
34. lucid dreaming god
35. 900 foot jesus
36. youtube laughing baby
37. youtube talking goat
38. channel 101 yacht rock
39. channel 101 jack black
40. channel 102
41. is new york better than los angeles
42. new york apartment swap
43. sixth borough
44. four hour work week
45. wiki random article
46. yentl
47. barbara oprah white mic
49. amy irving (Google images)
50. your name (again)

CHAPTER TWO:
HEAPING

GET
SHIT
DONE

Three Heaps

The best method for processing what you've gathered is the method you know you'll use. After amassing my stuff, I run a tight ship. I process my inbox every two to three years, sorting first into three categories according to size, shape, and odor:

Heap 1 (Heap of Consequence)
Heap 2 (Heap of Ambiguity)
Heap 3 (Heap of Miscellany)

I sort each Heap according to the layout of my office/breakfast nook/bedroom. Heap 3 goes near the door, and just spills out enough to keep the door from opening or closing very well. Heap 2 goes on the 'desk', which is actually a space on the floor where I keep pens, paperclips, white out, etc. Heap 1, where my urgent actions are filed, goes on the bed, and at night is transferred directly in front of my door so I can't leave without consciously avoiding it.

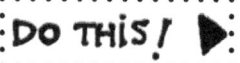 **Sort into Three Heaps**

Once in Heaps, the processing gets really exciting! From there, I put a sticky note on each object and sort into two piles:

- **To-Do**
- **To Not-Do**

To Not-Do's get sorted into paper, plastic, compost, and garage storage for yet-to-be-conceived grandchildren. To-do's then get sorted into two piles according to degree of time-sensitivity:

- **Freakout**
- **Chillax**

Every item in the freakout pile is then transferred onto a Triptych of Triumph list to make rock-solid sure it'll get done. Anything in the Chillax pile gets sorted again into two categories:

- **Need to Look Like I Have Shit Together**
- **Whatev's**

GSD Basic Processing Supplies:

-scotch (and the tape)
-file folders (different trash cans)
-UNloaded starter gun (to safely recreate the scene in Fight Club with the guy at the convenience store--really kick yourself into gear)
-colored pieces of paper to separate small pieces of paper
-nuts, power bars, protein shake
-first-aid kit
-steel-toed shoes/boots
-prayer book (denomination unimportant)

SORTING OPTIONS:

COLOR   SHAPE   ODOR

FIRE HAZARD   REFERENCE

Being "At Choice"

Several times a day *I am inspired by fresh, irresistible ideas for new projects. I usually pick the most delicious one and spin it into a multi-faceted project requiring lots of time, energy, money, and people to execute it. I run with it for a week, two weeks, discuss and develop it with my friends and creative partners. Asses its potential for inspiring people, bring joy, developing my portfolio, my sense of self, and financial viability (never choose a project that rates high in every area--you might get overwhelmed by joy). I get a really intense high from dreaming up new shit to do. At one point in my life, I got frustrated with my inability to follow through on everything I thought of. I kind of gave up. I felt awkward and kind of embarrassed about the things I developed with people but didn't finish, and didn't want to be someone who broke promises. I didn't want to commit to anything. Over a number of years, my high anxiety about deciding which things to do morphed into my imagining that I couldn't actually do them. But at some point, my world began to bloom again, and still I want to do everything. I want to do standup, make movies, write books, have kids, do a solo show, act in films, do improv, paint, make pottery, help people grow and feel alive, and yet as I get older, I become more and more aware that I don't have time to do EVERYTHING. And that's why it's absolutely imperative that one thinks up lots of ideas and start lots* *of projects--the more you have to choose from, the better the chances of choosing projects truly worth investing in. So how do we choose what's really important and what's not? And how do we enjoy just being alive enough that what we're doing matters less than how we're doing it? Which people let us feel that way and which people distract us from what's really important? Which activities? Which environments? Which governments? Which foods?*

Your Parachute

So I found myself reading 'What Color is Your Parachute?' *This afternoon. "But Alicia," you say, "You must have your shit together like no one else, and get it done so easily now that you have overcome the hurdles. You have your own website and everything. Look at what you do! You make movies, you run circuses, you tell jokes to people who in turn laugh at those jokes, you edit TV shows, you write screenplays, you write and produce one-woman-shows! You're a model for those of us who were wondering what color our parachute was! Your parachute is probably very clearly a specific mauve and eggshell pinstripe! And I bet it never catches on fire when you fire up that heat thing that heats*

the air to make it go higher, and I also bet no one ever hides on the side of the basket and then climbs inside and tries to high-jack you and your briefcase of money as you make your ascent and great escape! I bet that never happens! What more could you possibly need to know that would be found in such a book at the parachute one?" I mention my prolific creative work because I'd like to let you know that sometimes what I do is successful, and sometimes it's not. I am not "one of those people" who is creative and effective. I simply do it, fear and all. And I say this to highlight that you (yes, you) bring your own gifts that desire expression, and there is nothing special about "people who do neat shit" that you do not possess as well, dear reader. Moreover, if you are one of those "people who do neat shit", but still don't consider yourself one because of any number of excuses, it's time to draw yourself back inside the circle of special people.

DO THIS! ▶ NEW JERSEY, FLORIDA, OHIO

OHIO: Only Handle It Once. Yeah, I guess that could be helpful, if you want to be uptight about it. But let's get creative. How about FLORIDA? Find Lots of Ridiculous Inane Data, Annihilate. MARYLAND? Manage All Really Yucky Letters and Notes Diligently. KANSAS. Keep Analyzing Now Stop And Sigh.

Synchronicity

Today I was working in a café next to another woman. A piece of paper slipped off her table and flew directly under my fingers. I gave her the paper back, and we laughed for a couple of minutes at what happened. "Hey, what was on that piece of paper?" "My to-do list." I laughed again.

 **In the Cards**

Are you ready to put the power of synchronicity into GSD? I'm going to suggest something radical. I want you to throw out your to-do list. I'm not kidding. Take it now, and tear it word from word. Every task you're supposed to finish, everyone you're supposed to call, the reminders for the thank you note to your boss for the raise, the birthday card for your niece, the electricity bill. Everything. Now put the pieces of paper in a bag along with your wrist watch, which represents your concept of time. 'There's never enough time,' we say, 'time is running out,' we insist, 'it's later than you think!' we cry.

Now get a hammer. Smash the watch and the paper. Break it up real good. Now put it in a top hat and set it aside. We'll come back to it later, but first I'd like you to pick a card.

Seriously, read on only if you've burned, shredded, or drowned your to-do list. And put it in a top hat. That's the card you want? You sure? Don't show it to me. Have you memorized it? Ok, put it back in the deck. No, face down. Good.

Now I want you to get a pen and a piece of paper. Do it. Seriously, do it. I want you to write down the three people you know personally who most inspire you. Now write down your three favorite activities. Now write three favorite times in your life.

And now write down the one thing they all have in common (e. g. The quality of 'gentleness'). I want you to write the opposite of that one thing (e. g. 'forcefulness'). And now, this is complicated, but I want you to write down the opposite of the opposite, without using the first word (let's say, 'allowing'). Put that aside for now.

Ok, have you ever experienced coincidence? Have you heard talk of the same book several days in a row, and subsequently found a copy of it on the sidewalk (my friend always finds the next Harry Potter book somewhere when she's ready to read it)? Have you run into a friend in a distant city? Randomly asked someone's birth date and found it was the same as your own?

Write down the first coincidence that comes to mind. Immediately and without thinking, write down what that coincidence signaled to you (e. g. 'my best friend called me at the same moment I picked up the phone to call her. The phone didn't even ring. From this I take that somehow we are connected in an unseeable way').

Now plug your answers into this equation: I am (allowing) that (we are all connected in an unseeable way). Make it grammatically correct so I don't look like a shlump. Just jam it together. Go ahead. I have a 5 o'clock show on a cruise ship.

Now I want you to take this equation, and put it in the top hat. Wave your hand and say, 'There are no coincidences! There are no coincidences! There are no coincidences!' Now, take out your piece of paper really dramatically as if it's your old smashed watch that's been magically transformed into this new thing.

Is this your card? No? No. It's today's to-do list.

Other People's Shit

One of the most effective forms of procrastination is to get someone else's shit done instead of your own. Unless you're getting paid to do it, you have no business getting anyone else's very personal shit done (After age three, no one should need help wiping. After age twelve, no one should need help orgizing.) You must be ruthlessly clear about whose shit is whose. The diagram to the right sheds light on this.

Have you noticed that their stuff is shit and your shit is stuff? God! Can you move your shit so I can put some of my stuff down?
    -George Carlin

Chapter Two **Heaping**

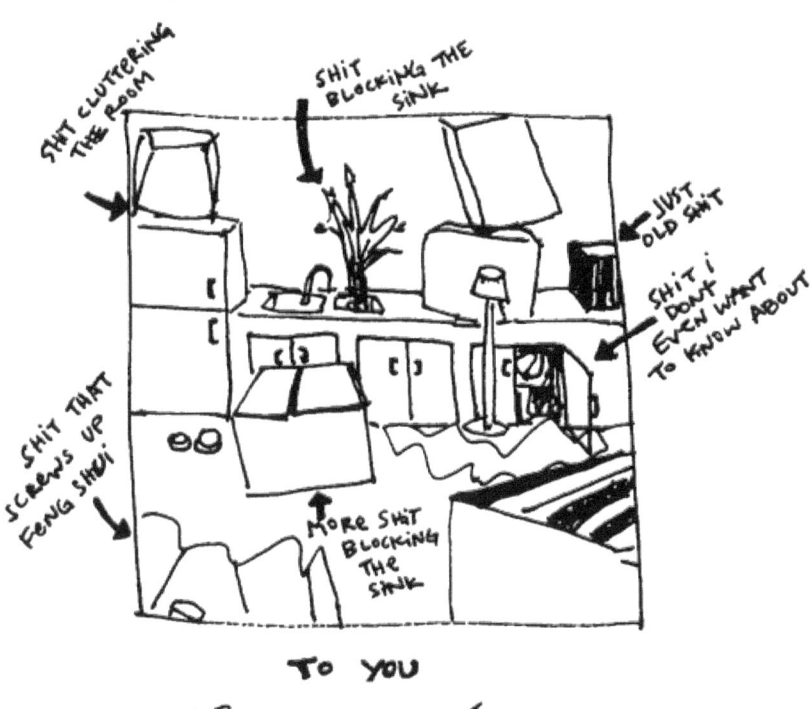

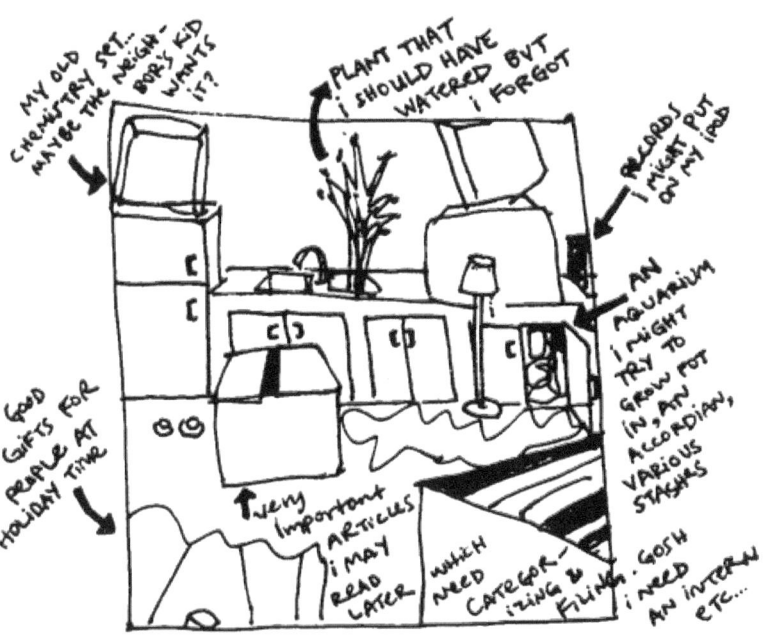

Getting Shit Done Tools For Unprofessionals

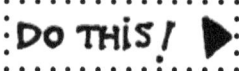 **Braintrapping**

Supplies: Notebook, pen, bush. To root out all open loops, you must act like a ruthless yet foolish cartoon character. The absolute best time to collect open loops (to empty the mind) is when you're trying not to think of them. Sit for 15 minutes per day in a quiet place and simply focus on the breath. Do your best to be still and clear your mind. Thoughts that have been waiting to escape for literally years will see this as a chance to make a break for it. Each time a thought arises, capture it in your notebook--enough to gather the idea, but not enough to take you away from your task. Then return to your meditation. The next day, take these thoughts and put them through your processing system. Are they "actionable"? Are they to-do someday? Are they dreams? Are they attacks or criticisms you need to defend yourself against..? Etc.

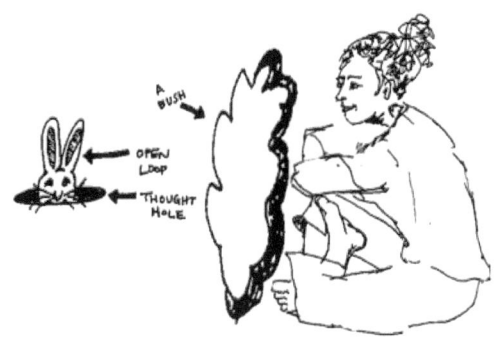

Above: Sit quietly behind a bush to wait for open loops to appear through the thought hole.

Chapter Two **Heaping**

I would now like to express the most vital concept of Getting Shit Done in the form of an interpretive dance, which I would now like to express in the form of a written essay.

Imagine a large dark room with a tiny luminous ball hanging from the ceiling. A creature clad in black with a face painted like a cloud awakens from a deep sleep. I am that creature. As I emerge from the blackness, I begin to limp. I am limping. I am injured. No, deformed. I raise my left hand to discover it is in fact a scientific calculator, and my right, an egg beater. Silently, I growl. My left foot is a baby alligator and on my right, an alligator boot. A jig begins to play. My alligator boot begins to jitterbug uncontrollably. Suddenly, I'm performing calculations with the egg beater. I growl again, my body rumbling as I am struck with a lightning bolt of advanced mathematical knowledge. I am performing the three-fingered mudras of Vecti (with an egg-beater—think Edward Scissorhands), Goddess of advanced mathematical knowledge, in the way one does when suddenly speaking and understanding Italian in a dream. We hear faint honking behind the jig, whose tune has grown loud and unwieldy, and now sounds more like a jig saw. The luminous ball grows brighter. I can now see

"Be vewy quiet. We're hunting wabbits."
 -Yosemite Sam

your faces clearly. You are smiling like flowers. The dark room, it turns out, is not a room at all. It is actually an alley in between three tall tenement buildings. Dogs are snarling, and paper is sprawling from last week's ticker tape parade. There is a clock and a stack of books. And a machine from a factory pressing plastic toys for Toy Story 3's release. I'm not really dancing anymore. Ok, it's a dance in which I inject plastic into little molds. When they cool, I take them out, put them in a bag, take them out of the bag excitedly, play with them, do a pee pee dance, and throw the plastic toy on the ground. Then I pick the toys up, 'smelt' them, inhale their fumes (get a little high), and inject the plastic back into the molds (still with the egg beater hand). I consult my card file. What's the next action? You are still smiling. No, now you are laughing. As quickly as it lit, the l u m i n o u s ball begins to fade until all you can see now is the cloud on my face. Perhaps it looks like a rubber ducky or the press secretary. No matter. I am still as a cloud.

Chapter Two **Heaping**

03

CHAPTER THREE:

PRETENDING TO ORGANIZE

GET SHIT DONE

Read Books on Organization

Why actually organize when you could just read books about it?

Getting Shit Done Tools For Unprofessionals

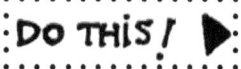 **Actual Helpful Suggestion**

How to have more time than you know what to do with: Don't check your email. That's it. I didn't check my email today. I worked on a poster, I edited some video, I looked up the weather. I didn't check my email. I met with a friend, I did some writing, I met with another friend, I did some reading, I ate some food, I went to work, I paid some bills, I played my ukulele, I called some friends, and I had SO MUCH TIME! As the day wore on, I found myself pulled more and more toward the email. It felt kind of like Yom Kippur (the one day every year Jews fast and pray all day and atone for our sins). Sort of holy, sort of empty, sort of reflective, sort of humbling. Every time I defeated the urge to check my email, I felt triumphant, and ready to take on the world, and maybe first check my email. Because I miss the spam. I miss getting hounded with a days worth of ads for cialis and hoodia and junk bonds. I miss knowing I clicked to saved the polar bear and the Alaskan wildlife and the First Amendment. I miss getting the lowdown about registering my cell phone on the do not call list. I miss the seven emails from the class clown in the comedy newsgroup who has to make fun of the spelling mistake in the last post. I miss those emails from people I never see and wouldn't call (because they lie just beyond that realm of relate-ability) who want to say a long lost hello. I miss clicking. I've never smoked a cigarette, but I imagine the act of clicking 'get mail' has a really similar effect on the brain. I guess with a cigarette, it's like you're always getting new mai*l*.

Momentary Purpose or Monetary Purpose?

The Art of GSD *is really about getting shit done so you can experience life. What are we trying to get at here? We're getting at letting go of the shit we didn't want to do in the first place but somehow felt obligated to in order to get to the shit we want to do. I like to ask myself, 'what's essential?' I like to ask myself this question on a regular basis, and be brutally honest and yet deeply compassionate with myself at the same time (which I'm about to do for you now, because I'm an artist and I consider it my job to expose my thought process to the light of day for various reasons).*

So why am I doing what I'm doing at this moment? What's the purpose of this action? How am I feeling at this moment? What's the purpose of this feeling? (Right now, I'm thinking, maybe people will read it and identify with it and like me. And what's the purpose of that? If they like me, will I then feel ok? Nope. Won't change anything. Ok, then is the writing of this worth doing in itself?) I don't change anything. I just ask. The other day  *I went to Rainbow Grocery to get some fruit-sweetened chocolate malt balls and some lunch. It was very important.*

It was in the middle of my day. I needed to eat, but did I need to go all the way to Rainbow? How much writing time did I use on that trip? I still went. This is what's new: I was conscious. And I didn't even eat the malt balls until yesterday. And fuck, they were fruit-sweetened. Can I get any healthier?

Brainstorming vs. Shitstorming

There are a lot of new terms and hype over brainstorming these days... mind-mapping, thought-thwapping, head-jamming. Some companies have their executives shouting out their fears while on a ropes course, some have them smoking pot and laying on yoga mats on the office floor to brainstorm. It's a competetive market place, and every "funsultant" has his or her own brand of innovation stimulation.

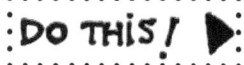 **How to Shitstorm**

The key is not to over-complicate the process. Think of an idea, write it down. Think of another one, write it down. On the opposite page is a diagram on capturing your brilliant ideas. If your creative process takes an ugly turn, don't throw the brainstorm out with the bathwater; save it and call it a shitstorm.

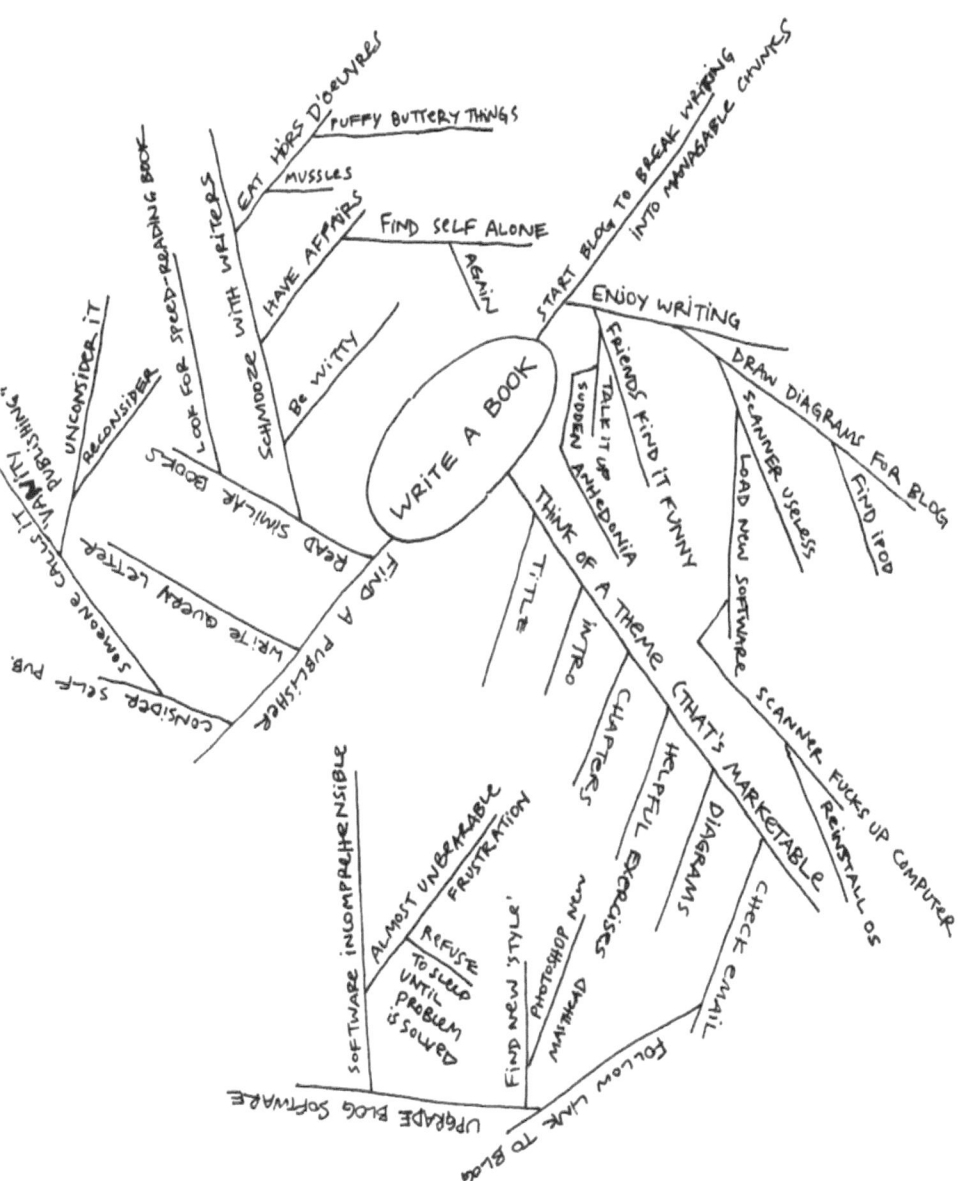

Capturing and Recording Everything

The next step in the system is to capture and record everything you have left in your inbox. Essentially, you take all of your important shit and write it down so you don't have to keep it in your head any more. The more you capture on paper, the more space is left in your brain for yummy new thoughts. Never mind that Greek schoolchildren memorized the Odyssey (33,333 lines of poetry). They must not have been able to remember what they ate for dinner!

 **Pick your Poison**

I compare several mechanisms of cataloguing your information in the diagram to the right. Of course there are these new fangled phones that keep your information automatically synced like the Blackberry and the iPhone as well. I'll address them in a future chapter in depth. But have you ever tried to fix a syncing problem with one of these things? It's like a black hole of timesucking. If you could capture the time you wasted syncing a phone to a computer, you could turn the clock back to your parents' youth.

Chapter Three **Pretending to Organize**

ELECTRIC PDA

vs.

- might lose stylus
- have to learn how to use
- needs charging
- breakable
- software goes out of date
- syncs to your computer, (wastes time)
- you might play games on it, waste more time
- fun to steal

HIPSTER PDA

vs.

- needs pen
- needs 3 x 5 cards

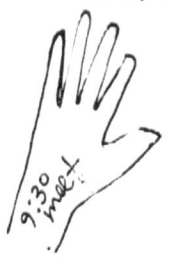

ULTRAHIP PDA

- smudges

Getting Shit Done Late at Night

It's midnight. The metaphorical kids are asleep in their imaginary beds. The metaphorical bone is hanging out of the dog's metaphorical mouth dripping with hypothetical saliva. Illusory husbands and wives are fake fast asleep, snoring and dreaming of calorie-free coffee heath bar ice cream. At long last you are alone, and with a sense of dread, you move toward the solemn tasks collected in the last several weeks.

You write a check for health insurance, begrudgingly noting that your policy has increased in cost by 88% in the last four years. You inwardly squeal with small delight in your first GSD triumph of the day. A bill paid. And, using for the first time a sticker with your address on it, greatly increasing your efficiency. That's perhaps 30 seconds of writing you can deposit directly in your Time Bank ™. Absolutely free time, or as I like to call it, discretionary time.

How to you save in your time bank? 2 in 1 shampoo and conditioner? Save customer service calls for commute hours? Say goodbye to energy vampires? Pretend you only need six hours of sleep? Skip boring sentences in bedtime stories?

How do you spend that discretionary time?

Chapter Three **Pretending to Organize**

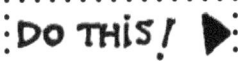 **The Cyclone Method**

There are methods for especially effective organization which seem counter-intiutive. This one works by putting everything in the wrong place and then throwing away whatever looks out of place. Magic.

The more dispersed, the better. As you work, write notes and spread them around your desk. Then, use a legal pad, sometimes. The fold the pages over often. Fill notebooks with disparate info. Scatter receipts so there's always one somewhere when you need a piece of scrap paper or toilet paper or a place to put your gum.

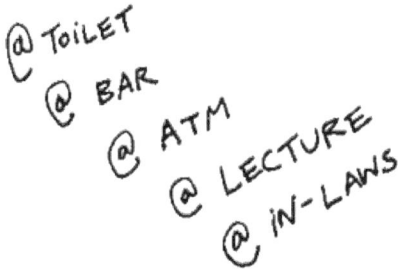

 **@ Lists**

I like the Zen-Like Paralysis state. But if you don't it's good to shield your pretty little head from everything you have to get done so your mind doesn't go all pins and needles. Write what you have to do on separate lists and only consult the list if you're in that place.

Do you have what it takes?

Discipline. Courage. Passion. Gentleness. Persistence. Self-knowledge. *Do you possess these qualities? Do you have the discipline every day not to get shit done? It takes a lot of work not to write, not to go to the post office, not to set goals. You have to constantly keep anesthetizing yourself. The internet, the peanut butter, the room-cleaning, the pushups. The peanut butter.*

Think big. Fail even bigger. Do you have the courage to fail? A study found it takes the average person 11 attempts to quit smoking cigarettes. Do you have the courage to start smoking again 10 times to achieve your goal of freedom?

Are you fierce? Can you breathe fire into a goal which, in the grand scheme of things, is utterly meaningless? Your dream of building and racing toothpick sailboats will likely be scorned and belittled by overbearing bosses, inane co-workers, bewildered strangers, well-meaning friends, concerned family members, and curious ducks. Not to mention the voices in your own head. Can you, season after season, oh maker of meaning, draw strength from the goddesses and gods of sailing and toothpicking to find your true path in this

Chapter Three **Pretending to Organize**

watery world?

Are you gentle? When (oh, right… I mean, if) your boat sinks, will you push back the tears, or will you let them gently stream down your face, crying, "I have failed miserably and brilliantly, and I am more alive than ever!" Or will you do the other thing you used to do (fill in your own blank)?

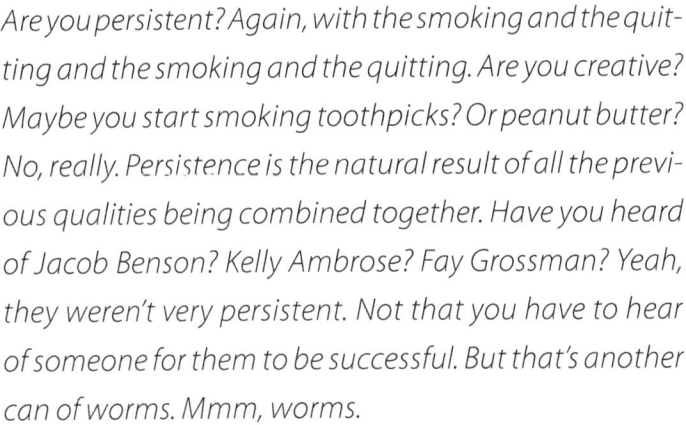

Are you persistent? Again, with the smoking and the quitting and the smoking and the quitting. Are you creative? Maybe you start smoking toothpicks? Or peanut butter? No, really. Persistence is the natural result of all the previous qualities being combined together. Have you heard of Jacob Benson? Kelly Ambrose? Fay Grossman? Yeah, they weren't very persistent. Not that you have to hear of someone for them to be successful. But that's another can of worms. Mmm, worms.

Person, know thyself! I've gotten to know myself very well. I know I should go to bed at 10 or 11 pm. It's 1 am now. I get tired. I eat too much. I wash dishes. I start new projects. And I've got to get up early. However, I know this about myself: I really like to write at night. So I sacrificed a bit of sleep for this toothpick sailboat. And now I am happy.

How Ironic (or not) *that in the writing of this book,*

I'm sitting at my computer, procrastinating doing something else! Yet, it happens to all of us. This chapter might be shitty. Why? Because I don't want to write it now. I want to write it later. But I'm doing it anyway. Because I've committed myself to the work. Regardless of what I feel like doing right now, I'm doing this anyway. Ok, the truth is that it's 1:30 am and I didn't write all day, and I was about to go to sleep and write a chapter in the morning about how it's ok to slip and not do something you're committed to as long as you can forgive yourself and begin again. But this is a better way. Do it even when you "don't feel like it". Because in the big picture, you do want to Get Shit Done, and "not feeling like it" is just resistance. Oh, plus I ate two chocolate chip cookies an hour ago to put this off, and it didn't work-I'm doing it anyway.

Dealing With Resistance

Disorganized objects and information are only on the surface of not getting shit done. There's something powerful behind disorganization. Maybe you're feeling resistant to even hearing or believing this... What's behind your resistance? Try these exercises when you're feeling stuck:

Time is a great teacher. Unfortunately it kills all its pupils.
-Hector Berloiz

Chapter Three **Pretending to Organize**

DO THIS! ▶ **Doing the Unstuck**

1) Take some deep breaths from the belly
2) Write down what's in your way: (twist comes here)
3) Write down a list of things you're grateful for (twist)
4) Write down a list of your assets (twist)
5) Get back to work

The Downward Spiral

So let's cut to the quick. Is your shit wrecking your life? Get rid of it. When you look around your office, your bedroom, your kitchen, do you see each object as a representative of an opportunity to live more deeply and fully reinforcing your passion, or a dream deferred, weighing on your soul and reminding you of past failures and shortcomings?

Calling Forth Your Fucking Warrior

Ask yourself these three questions when considering if some shit is wrecking your life:

1) Do I use this shit every day?
2) Does this shit sitting in my (location) make my life better?
3) Does this shit fit with the vision of highest self?

How honest were you with yourself? Were you a little bit truthless? Well, it's time to take the t-bag out and get ruthless. (Yes, I just wrote that whole sentence for comic self-help effect. Imagine you were watching a motivational speaker with a Powerpoint presentation and he just animated the "t" in truthless getting smashed into little pieces.)

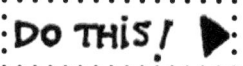 **Make two heaps:**

Opportunity for Passionate Living	Trigger for Downward Spiral
cheap ukulele	fancy guitar
Gabriel Garcia novel	Nietzsche you didn't finish
new kitchen knife	new PS3

This exercise is all gut, no brains. Objects represent something that our minds don't comprehend. We feel in our guts. Do you want to live in a museum of dead dreams? Get rid of all that shit in heap two.

Now, write your shitlist. Everything you've been holding back on, putting off, fearing, procrastinating. What are you really afraid of? What have you made that mean? You don't have to act on any of it, but get it all on paper so you can see it.

Now evaluate each thing. Is it scary? Hard? What?

Now take action on something in your list.

Fuckit Files (Trash-Based)

Once you've captured your information, you'll need to store it. David Allen has this system whereby you store things by day of the month, and then by month (adding up to 43 folders, hence the website 43folders.com), and then there's a pending file and a "tickler" file (for tickly things? feathers? Elmo?). I find all that filing to be a huge timesuck. My Fuckit Files are always in style. Too much in the file? Throw it in the trash file! See diagram below to properly set up your file system.

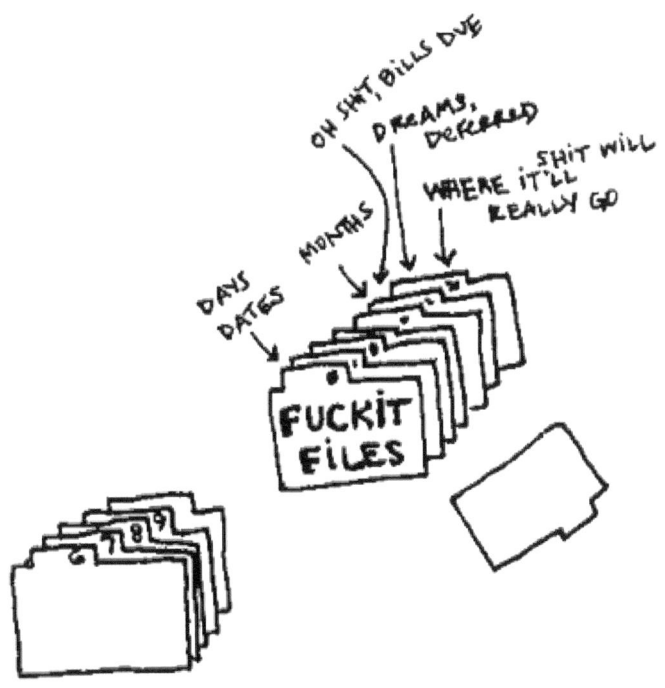

The Upward Spiral

You're never in the same place you were before, even if it feels familiar. This pint of ice cream I ate in bed last night is different than the others. I still ate it, but I felt 1% or 6% less compelled to do so and 15% to 20% less guilty about having done so afterward. It was not so bad. It's like losing the superbowl by 2 points this time instead of 20. Or losing the election to fraud and violation of civil liberties and impossibly unfair campaign finance laws rather than just plain ignorance or shitty candidates. Imagine this: if you only made a 1% shift each day in how you do or percieve something you want to change, you can shift 100% in just over three months!

Chapter Three **Pretending to Organize**

04

CHAPTER FOUR:

THE CONTINUING HEADACHE

GET SHIT DONE

Synapping--Take a Nap!

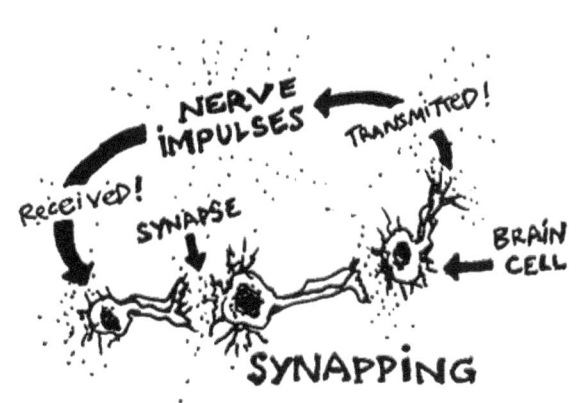

While some brain fitness experts recommend "stimulating" and "challenging" the brain's synapses with "strenuous mental activity" to increase brainpower, genius Albert Einstein said that his best ideas came in the twilight between waking and sleeping (just at the moment the brain's alpha waves dip). Einstein would sit on a chair holding weights in his hands when he was sleepy, and as he began to fall asleep, the weights would start to fall and wake him up. It was in this way that he accessed this subconscious world of creativity.

Have you noticed that you are funniest, smartest, or most creative unintentionally? It is said that the subconscious mind is seven years ahead of the subconscious mind--the more we access the unconscious mind, the deeper the well we have to tap.

DO THIS! ▶ Sleepsorting: Take another Nap!

Dream your way to the top. Sleeping and dreaming are powerful tools. The unconscious brain uses this time to re-organize thoughts, process events, and sort ideas. To harness your unconscious brainpower, save your last waking five minutes to set out your most complex problems. Review and put on paper in front of you what's most irking, frustrating, or blocking you. For example, "How can I make the rent this month?" Allow it to look really messy. Let yourself get really worked up. The more you signal your brain that this is something you want to process, the better the process will work. When you

> *"A journey of a thousand miles begins with a single step."*
> *-Confucius*

Chapter Four **The Continuing Headache**

reach the upper limit of emotional tolerance, tell yourself three times, "Show me a way to resolve this problem." Then quickly turn out the light and fall asleep. (If you can't sleep, you probably haven't worked the process hard enough–it may take several weeks of practice.)

Immediately upon waking, pen some notes on your dreams directly next to the previous night's problems. Your dreams about tap dancing sideways with a video camera and discussing the movie Ghost with an older female friend will undoubtedly shed light on your financial woes, but the next and final step is crucial. Renowned dream expert Jeremy Taylor says we all have a 'blindness' to the most valuable insights of our dreams. He suggests a method of collective projective dreamwork whereby one allows a group of people to use their collective imagination to help interpret the dream's meanings. Your brain knows exactly what to tell you and exactly when, so use what you've learned during the night to solve what's been bugging you. I've found the best groups to help interpret dreams are not necessarily friends. Your co-workers, unbiased and disinterested,

"Walk this way."
-Aerosmith, Run DMC

will be the most beneficial group in helping elucidate insights. Pick a time of the day when you're all together, like an early business meeting, or a company luncheon to share the tap dancing images and let the insights begin!

Cultivate Cerebral Hypoefficiency

As it turns out, my brain has been mush for the last ten years. I only found this out on Saturday. I decided to read a book a day for the next couple of weeks (half a week has gone by and I've read more books now than I read in the last half a year). Saturday I read a book called Brain Fitness. Apparently, having avoided advanced mathematics courses, crossword puzzles, rigorous anything (ok, I took a rhetoric course at UC Berkeley just for the hell of it), I've cultivated a state of cerebral hyopefficieny that only happens when people retire. And perhaps all the thinking and obsessing I was doing was just the perverted response my healthy brain had to the lack of intellectual stimulation since high school. I realize now that my mind has felt like the driver of a race car, stuck in a closed parking lot, stifled, resorting to peeling out and those sideshows kids do in the streets in Oakland.

Brain Fitness has a test for people who are "getting up in years" to tell if they've got cerebral hypoef-

Chapter Four **The Continuing Headache**

ficiency (flabhead). Most of their questions involve where you put your keys. It's true though that the mind needs stretching as much as the calves. Have you become a flabhead?   Score yourself in this informal quiz:

Flabhead Test

DO THIS ! ▶

I often forget where I put my keys:	**yes no**
I shy away from scrabble becuse I can't remember a lot of words:	**yes no**
I am the only one of my friends who wasn't a Sudoku freak:	**yes no**
I listen to the news, but I couldn't tell you what's actually happening today:	**yes no**
I rely completely on my cell phone for phone numbers and on caller id to recognize who is calling:	**yes no**
When the check comes, I need a pen to figure out the tip:	**yes no**
I've cultivated trust and forgiveness toward strangers just so I don't have to count my change when shopping:	**yes no**

I've cultivated kindness and inquisitiveness toward strangers because most strangers are actually people whose name or face I've forgotten: **yes no**

Holding a conversation without access to Google is a strain: **yes no**

0 yes: Your brain is fit as a fiddle! (Or you forgot to count up the yes's, and this is worse than misplacing your keys because it just happened now.) You likely seek out new experiences to stimulate you daily and engage in your world in an exciting and lively way! Congratulations.

1-2 yes: A bit of flab. A little brain-nip and tuck is all you need. Take a class, tackle some good books, and don't ignore it (like I am!).

3-5 yes: Proust said that this kind of laziness leads to depression and illness. Pull your brain up by your bootstraps, dammit.

all yes: It's likely you're the sort of person that reads books like "Brain Fitness" and buys software for your computer like the "Brain Gym", but rarely make use of them. It's therefore likely you're having a recur-

ring problem with change. If so, you need to do repeated bushwacking--continual building
of new neuronal pathways to reinforce the shift in consciousness and shift in identity to recreate yourself as a person who succeeds and enjoys positive things. Attempt change in very small increments and show yourself you can succeed by doing even something new one minute per day. When you get to one minute per day for three weeks, build on that. Fight cerebral hypoefficiency. Don't waste another minute reading this drivel. Get out and do something meaningful to you!

Paradoxical Efficiency of Indecision

I use a lot of 3 x 5 cards. to throw at annoying people who seem to be getting more done than me. If you spin them at just the right angle, you can give a wicked paper cut. I also use them to leave notes on people's cars when they're taking up two spaces in a parking lot, I'm feeling pent-up and want to kick the metaphorical dog.

How It Really Works:

The cornerstone of Getting Shit Done is the PARADOXICAL EFFICIENCY OF PROCRASTINATION AND INDECISION. Take a 3 x 5 card and write down three things I call the:

DO THIS! ▶   Triptych of Triumph:

•an impossible multi-phase action (e. g. lose six pounds this week)
•an unreasonable abstract expectation (e. g. 'I should be a better guitarist by now, but I can't get myself to practice the damn scales')
 •a mundane concrete task (e. g. pick up dry-cleaning)

The impossibility of completing the first two tasks makes the third task appear utterly simple.

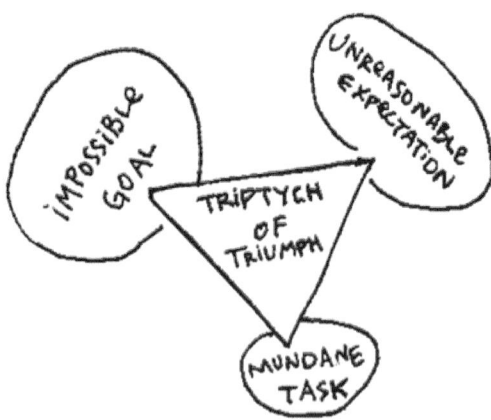

Studies show the barrage of 21st century communication sends us continually in and out of varying degrees of post-traumatic stress disorder. One minute we're on-track and unpredictably reeling the next. By jolting the mind solidly back into trauma with an impossible action and an unreasonable expectation, we actually bypass the frontal lobe and route the only clear action possible (dry-cleaning) directly to the nervous system. Years of experimentation developed this system, and I've taught myself to implement it so efficiently that I pick up other people's dry-cleaning.

Abstract Goals

Did you know that scientists have recently been able to observe the same particle in two locations at once? The fabric of space and time is mysterious. Physicists theorize that there are an infinite number of dimensions and hence infinite possibilities. Only at the moment of choice do our possibilities shrink from infinite to singular. So why choose?! Setting concrete goals locks us into a concept of what it is to get shit done. It sets us up to see a dualistic reality: black/white, start/finish, succeed/fail, cat/dog. And we often choose to feel good or bad depending on whether we succeed or fail.

DO THIS! ▶ Concrete and Abstract Goals

Take a moment to write down several concrete goals you've been considering, e. g. fix head gasket, load cd library onto ipod, earn PhD.

In a second column, write the steps and the time it will take to get that shit done. Then imagine how you would feel completing your goals versus how you would feel never completing them and write about it in a third column.

Now, formulate an abstract goal, e. g. appreciate old friend, feel love for pet, enjoy new hair style. How would you feel accomplishing these goals? Now take five minutes and do them. I just got all that shit done.

Imagine how much shit we could get done if we decided to do different shit!

> *It is a fine thing to be a walking encyclopedia of philosophy, but if you happen to have no liking for philosophy, and to have a liking for the natural history of street-cries, much better to leave philosophy alone, and take to the street-cries.*
> 		-Arnold Bennett

DO THIS! ▶ Who are you?

Positive ego identification is not only healthy, it's vital if we are to even consider enlightenment. How can you dissolve an ego if you don't have one yet?

Through a series of inquires, let's examine who you think you are. Are you someone who gets shit done?

1) Describe your current self-image
2) Write out the highest vision of what you want your life to be.

Stake Your Claim.

Remember Other People's Shit? Let's re-visit that. The sooner you stake your time out, the more shit you'll get done. When you talk to a financial advisor, they'll tell you take the money you make and put the first chunk into savings. You pay yourself FIRST. Then you pay bills. Then you buy things. When you talk to a flight attendant, they'll tell you to put the oxygen mask on your own face first, then your child's. When it comes to time, give yourself the oxygen mask. It won't inflate, but it's still working.

If you are constantly getting other people's shit done, you'll forsake your own.

Getting Shit Done Tools For Unprofessionals

DO THIS! ▶ Put a Stake in It

Make a list of things that are just for you. These will be the "no-matter-what else I will do this thing for myself" things. The mind may wander into territory of others and what they need--bill-paying, which if they're your bills, doesn't count for you-time. Continue regardless of the distracted mind. You are teaching it to take time for yourself. Let nothing and no one stand in the way of this time. I always think of it like the oxygen masks in the airplane. As the adult, you always have to put your oxygen mask on first before you put your kid's mask on. That way, you'll be there to take care of her no matter what. I think that's how it works. That, or they just think adults' lives are more important. Anyway, here are some examples:

You Time: meditating, writing, jogging, playing, eating, etc.

Everyone Else Time: bill paying, emailing, phone calling, putting on kids' oxygen masks, etc.

Me, Inc.

Want to be the kind of person who gets shit done? Surround yourself with others who do the same (if you can find them--they're probably not hanging out at the cafe). Who are your "board members"? Psychologists say

Chapter Four The Continuing Headache

if you want to know who you are and what you think of yourself, look at the five people you spend the most time with. (They say also that your top five closest people also reflect the kind of money you're likely to make. But that's another book.) So who are your top five? Are they kind? Passionate? Awake? How do they see you? If you want to become a more productive person (or any other kind of person), consciously choose the people who you are close to.

DO THIS! ▶ Your Top Five

1) List the five people you spend the most time with, and describe them.
2) List the five people in the world you'd like to be influenced by most. Ghandi? MLK? The Dalai Lama? Oprah?
3) Look at the difference between this list. Disparage.
4) Find new friends?
5) Talk to mom less?

Learn a bit more about yourself by reflecting on some "example people" (ok, they're the example people are actually cardboard cut-outs I made to be my friends. Don't judge.) **Which example person's top five is closest to your own?**

Person A
1) financial advisor
2) husband
3) best-selling author
4) senator
5) baby sitter
6) (baby)

    Person B
    1) therapist
    2) massage therapist
    3) sponsor
    4) acupuncturist
    5) health food store girl who sells vitamins

        Person C
        1) weed dealer
        2) pizza guy
        3) lesbian ex-girlfriend
        4) substitute teacher buddy
        5) guitar dude

            Person D
            1) professional magician
            2) IT guy
            3) IT guy
            4) IT guy
            5) professional wrestler
                (I know, weirdo, right?)

Chapter Four **The Continuing Headache**

05

CHAPTER FIVE:
TAKING (NON) ACTION

GET SHIT DONE

05

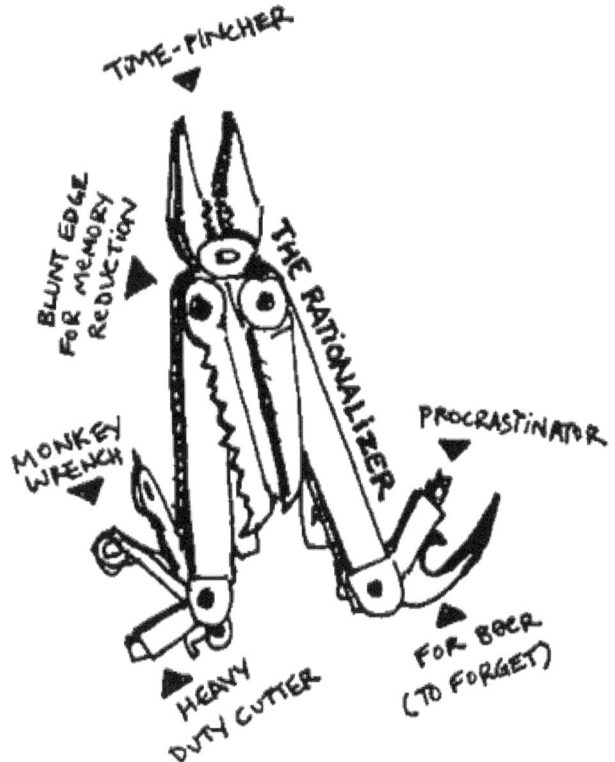

Rationalization: Leatherman of Procrastination

Regardless of your IQ, you are already a genius at rationalization. Here's how to put it to work for you. This tool works best for the tough stuff. Don't use it on errands like going to the post office or walking the dog--that'd be like giving a child Crystale when table wine would suffice.

It can actually be a fun activity to create rationalizations for tasks you don't even have to do yet! And remember, be ruthless with yourself. The following rationalizations will help get your started. You can, of course write ones on your own that really sound authentic to you.

DO THIS! ▶ Fun Rationalizations!

-For not getting to work on time:
    "Nobody else is on time either!"
    "Who are they to boss me around? My time is important, too."
    "I have to finish my yoga, and no boss-man is going to get in the way of my health and well-being. Besides, I'll be a more productive worker if I do my yoga."

-For not calling your grandmother:

"She's old, and she probably doesn't remember how long it's been since I called anyway."

"She wants me to be happy and healthy, and if I have to hear her nagging, I'm going to get sad and ill."

"I'm hungry and I might pass out if I don't get something to eat."

-For not writing the next chapter of the book:

"Maybe the book is done."

"Maybe it's a stupid idea."

"Maybe it won't even get published anyway."

"Maybe it's too self-referential."

"Maybe there are more important things to do than write a book, like cuddle babies, or work for world peace, or make a shitload of money."

"Maybe I should wash my car. Again."

"Maybe the kitchen needs painting."

"I spent the whole morning putting in a comma--and the whole afternoon taking it out again."

-Oscar Wilde

Completion

Like there's some project you've had hanging over your head for centuries, and somehow it's never finished? I remember (and have perhaps distorted) an old wives' tale about fisherman's wives who would sew sweaters for their husbands at sea–but right before they got to the end, they'd unravel the thing and start over again– because if they finished the sweater and he was at sea, it meant he was dead. Like my circus. That was a fun project. So many people collaborated. Getting to work and play with the infamous Benjamin Turner (who is now on tour with the Carpet Bagger Brigade) was a dream come true (nightmare? Just kidding, Ben). But, fuck, it took a year to plan and a year to execute. And another six months to make the tour movie. And it's all out of sync and I have to re-cut it. It's still not done!

Perfectionism. A major obstacle to GSD.

How do we know when to stop working on a piece of art (a film, a short story, an ice carving)? It's like dating. You gotta check yourself. I've adapted the dating protocol to art. When I don't know what to do in a relationship, I call friends who know me, tell the truth, and ask for their perspective. And I put that information on the table. I talk to the person and tell them where I'm at. I meditate on it. I sleep on it. I read about it. I write about it. I make art about it.

Chapter Five **Taking (Non) Action**

Which brings us back to the art. e. g. I've been ramping up my standup writing. And I had the bright idea to create a Filemaker database to put all my ideas into so I wouldn't lose them as easily. It's also helpful to be able to sort them by topic for when I want to build longer sets. And I could even go back through my old notebooks and harvest the old seeds I sowed long ago! But then my mind said, "Hold the fuck on–you're going to buy Filemaker Pro, load it on to the computer, build a database, go through all your old notebooks, and then write new jokes? That's a couple of weeks' work and you might lose the steam you had to write jokes in the first place inside a steam-sucking computer chamber! NO WAY." And then another voice said, "MAKE A PHONE CALL to someone who has PERSPECTIVE." So I called my comedy mentor (who knows how I work and how I shirk my work), told him the story, and he said "DO IT!" So I'm doing it. In the past, I would have spent a week just puzzling over whether to make the stupid database and not written a single joke. I saved a week with one phone call. Ah, progress. And as for getting a project "stick-a-fork-in-it" done? Not gonna happen. Maybe for dead people. My good friend Brian's motto is helpful for perfectionists (but not for imperfectionists): "Better done than good." Am I wondering to myself, 'Is this section good enough?'

"Better done than good."
-Brian Doherty

Yes. Am I willing to stay up until 4:30 am again to perfect it? No.

Procrastination: The Stealth Weapon of GSD

Do you believe that there are uber-organized geniuses whose sheer throughput you will never surpass? Yeah, I guess there are. But you and I, we've got the next best thing: the secret weapon of procrastination. Ever try to get one thing done all day, like writing a business plan, avoid it for hours and hours on end, and subsequently get 18 other things done instead?

I just installed a keyboard tray, cleaned my apartment, cleaned out two closets and sorted out two boxes of crap to go to goodwill, worked out at the gym, met with two clients, answered ALL of my email, and worked on my website. All under the ominous threat of writing a business plan. Everybody that gets anything done has a secret procrastination weapon. You think Bill Gates just gets shit done cause he's perky? No! He's probably expected by his down-to-earth wife to take the garbage out at home, and he's a neat-freak and has to organize his ties by color, texture, and pattern if he's left to himself with free time, so he goes to work all day just to avoid it, and earns three billion dollars, so he can pay the housekeeper to do it.

Shock Value

Why file all of your reminders and action lists in one place when you could find the right place for each one? Do you keep your toothbrush in your Pending file in order to remember to brush? No. They why would you keep your call list anywhere but by the phone? Or your...?

The mind works best when alert. I like to stay alert by continually surprising myself. Sometimes I'll set an alarm in the middle of the night just to keep myself on my toes. I like to put post it notes in unexpected places throughout the house reminding me of random things that need doing. Write notes on your toaster, on your windshield, under your pillow. You can even use sticky notes to stay inspired.

DO THiS! ▶ Organizational Affirmations

Choose some of these phrases or write some of your own, put them on stickies and post them all over your home.

"Every day I become more and more organized."
"I file and feel complete."
"The more I file, the higher I vibrate."
"Time is my friend; I call her by her first name,

Kelly."

"When I align with Spirit, all files are in perfect order."

"My inner child intuitively knows how to stay organized."

"Out of silence and stillness, the mess falls away."

Incremental Regression

I love starting projects. The brainstorming. The new ideas springing forth like Athena from Zeus. The world rolling out at my feet. Wind in my hair. Everything opens up. There's a palpable sense of possibility. The sun breaks through the clouds. Nothing can stop me. Except the next step of the project (but I'll address this discursively).

And there are a lot of ideas out there. Some fall away (or get shot down by well-meaning friends–never tell people your unhatched ideas), some you nurse and coo into being, and others seem to arrive fully-

formed and raise themselves. Choosing to support the project whose brilliance shines through you is wise. The strength of the project and of your conviction will naturally attract the generous assistance of others, and we want to be part of something bigger.

So you choose a project. Wind in hair. High as a kite. Etc. It's likely you'll eventually hit a point of resistance. What happens then? You and your big ideas. You dreamer, you. What were you thinking? All the right things. Just too fast. And it's dangerous when you're that high.

So I've spent a lot of years with big ideas. And turned a few of them into big projects. And struggled with frustration and resistance and doubt. And I've discovered a secret. The best way I've found to bring an idea to fruition is to move in (almost imperceptible) increments with unshakable dedication to the smallest of efforts. Try these!

DO THIS! ▶ Two Steps Forward...

Example: eating one dozen donuts in a sitting. You can't do that shit all at once. You start with a bite a day. Within a few weeks, you could be eating dozens of donuts per day. Mmm, heart attack.

Example: you aspire to cover your entire house with small colorful sticky dots for a very large game of finger Twister. Whee!

Example: one day you could hold the world's record

for the most jumps on a pogo stick.

Example: worldwide nuclear disarmament and ensuing reign of peace.

Example: thinking of a lot of examples.

Example: learning Esperanto. Actually, that's dumb. Don't bother.

Slow and steady. Slow and steady.

The Power of Payday.

Imagine a world in which your productivity increases exponentially according to your pay-scale. When your eight-hour workday yields not only a paycheck but also a full day's work of your own. It can be a reality. Become a supervisor. A night watchman. A news editor. A librarian. A boss. A job that offers a level of downtime.

Get a bohemian day job that involves patiently sitting on your ass most of the day. Work during work! Take your fat action list and coordinate it so that work errands coincide with your errands. Faxing. Post office. Down time work: photocopying, emailing, job searching, scheduling, journaling, joke-writing, catching up on news, blogging, freelance writing, working on a book. Stay up

POWER OF PAYDAY

late getting your own shit done. Why should your boss get the most productive hours of your morning?

DO THIS! ▶ **"Working" at Work**

Here are some tips to create the appearance of productivity:

-Avoid Facebook, Twitter, etc.
-Avoid the position illustrated above
-Keep TV/iTunes low
-Look serious, but not overly serious
-When making photocopies, (zine, etc.) Always look official and confident

From Multi-tasking to Ultra-tasking

Time-saving tips: Things to combine during your day to save time. Try to combine things with eating, because that always takes up a lot of time.

DO THIS! ▶ **Ultra-tasking**

- emailing and catching up with relatives
- flossing and showering
- cooking and exercising
- eating and shopping
- eating dinner and breakfast
- driving and doing pilates
- cleaning and exercising
- working and sleeping

From Delegating to Relegating

It can be helpful to hire a personal assistant, coach, or professional organizer to work with you to get organized. But consider this... why get someone else to do your shit when you could just not do it at all? Just a thought.

Chapter Five **Taking (Non) Action**

THE REAL VALUE OF GSD

GET
SHIT
DONE

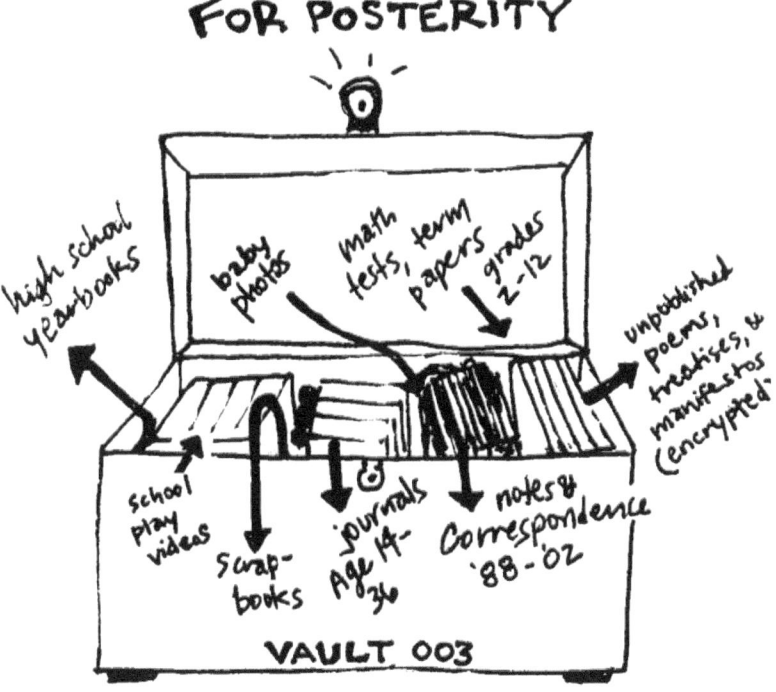

Posterity

I've spoken about how implementing GSD can bypass stumbling blocks, open side-doors for unexpected organization, and radically shift the way you navigate your day-to-day life. But there's one even greater application of GSD that I've been saving for last… what's MOST exciting about GSD:

A successfully integrated system will streamline the research process and fast-track your late-life or post-humous biography to the press.

Biographers, historians, and archeologists can literally spend years tracking down yellowing photos, work emails, fourth grade English tests, finger paintings, diaries, love letters, back taxes, possibly sentimental nic nacs, lists of old lovers, notes on inventions, screenplay drafts, and collected business cards to gain insight into the depth and breadth of your character. They need to get an idea of who you were, really. An annotated catalogue of all these items, as I keep in several fireproof trunks, will allow full interpretation of your life philosophy, evidence of having lived according to that philosophy, and given of yourself, and left a legacy, only partially in granite, for the People for generations, nay, centuries to come.

The Value of Emptiness

Now What? Directed focus at managing the endless stream of tasks, projects, and logistics necessarily calls into question what this drive is directed toward. The strength of what "matters" creates an equal opposite force of unseen "anti-matter". When you've achieved optimum organization, what will you do with it? Many people take this new skill and kick their lives into hyperdrive. If they were productive before, now they get six times as much done. They take on new projects, start businesses, take their lives to the next level. But be aware that that's not the only option--because it can happen simply by default--you empty your action list, and you find the need to do more with all your free time. Solution: sharpen the blade of choice. Decide exactly how much or how little you want to do, and then schedule anti-matter. If you're not ready to accept the value of emptiness, I will help you trick yourself. Zen action list. Wei wu wei ("Doing Not Doing").

DO THIS! ▶ **Doing Not Doing**

For the Beginner:

-eat fake fruit
-play air guitar (or air cat)

-walk imaginary dog on one of those wire leash

Intermediate Nothingness:

-set timer, measure shadows moving
-generate a fake shopping list of absurd things you can't buy, go to the store and try to buy them
-read book in a language you can't understand

Advanced Nothingness:

-stare into utter blank space
-schedule a fake workshop for the weekend, cancel it at the last minute
-go on a "mind-your-own-buisiness trip"--tell no one-- or if anyone asks where you're going, you can tell them, "Mind Your Own Business"
-read book in a language you can't understand

The Real Value of **GSD**

Getting Shit Done Tools For Unprofessionals

Don't ask yourself, "What does the world need?"
Ask yourself what makes you come alive.
Because what the world needs is people who have come alive.

-Howard Thurman

Getting Shit Done Tools For Unprofessionals

About the Author

Alicia Dattner, "Best Local Comedian 2011"-East Bay Express, is based in San Francisco. She leads workshops in humor and creativity, coaches clients, and speaks across the country about balance, purpose, and aliveness.

Alicia has directed several award-winning short films, toured the country with a circus she started, *The Latest Show on Earth* and acted in film and television.

Alicia's first one-woman-show, *The Punchline* recently won Best Female Act in the San Francisco Fringe Festival. Her show, *Eat, Pray, Laugh!* toured the country. It won a Goldstar Highest Member Rated Show Award and Best Storyteller at the NY United Solo Festival. Her newest show, *The Oy of Sex*, is in production.

You can visit her websites at :
www.alicadattner.com
www.creativeheartcoaching.com
www.oyofsex.com

Available from aliciadattner.com
(Visit the website for easy ordering.)

Eat, Pray, Laugh! DVD...$20

The Punchline DVD..$20

The Latest Show on Earth Circus **Tour DVD**.....$20

The Latest Show on Earth Circus **T-Shirts**..........$15

Getting Shit Done:
Productivity for Unprofessionals............................$15

www.ingramcontent.com/pod-product-compliance
Ingram Content Group UK Ltd.
Pitfield, Milton Keynes, MK11 3LW, UK
UKHW041958230426
12048UKWH00008B/401